Transcending
Boundaries

A Journey Through Transgender History

Adam J. Johnson

Contents

INTRODUCTION

Welcome to "Transcending Boundaries: A Journey Through Transgender History." In this informative and educational book, we travel on a transforming journey that transcends time, cultures, and geographies to examine the rich tapestry of transgender experiences. We dig into the historical, societal, cultural, and personal facets of transgender history, casting a light on the trailblazers, struggles, and victories that have influenced the transgender rights movement.

Embracing the Journey

Transgender history is a tribute to the tenacious spirit of individuals who have battled society boundaries and asserted their right to live truthfully. From ancient civilizations to the modern world, transgender people have been a vital part of the human experience, making an unmistakable mark on history. The journey begins with the realization that gender diversity is a timeless and necessary element of humanity.

Celebrating Gender Diversity in Ancient Notions

Our adventure begins by delving into ancient gender concepts, where we meet gender-nonconforming characters renowned for their spiritual understanding and revered as sacred beings. Gender variety has been acknowledged by diverse civilizations since ancient times, as seen by the acceptance of Two-Spirit individuals among Indigenous societies and the inclusion of transgender figures in myths around the world.

Resisting Oppression and Forging Paths

We see the beginnings of medicalization and pathologization of transgender identities as we travel through the Victorian and Edwardian eras. In this time of secrecy and repression, we honor the courage of transgender people who have bravely defied injustice, paving the way for greater visibility and acceptance.

Pioneering Transgender Activists and Advocates

Our journey celebrates the lives and achievements of trailblazing transgender activists and advocates who defied cultural obstacles, battled for legal recognition, and advocated for equality. From the mid-twentieth century to the present, their tales inspire us to be change agents and allies in the fight for transgender rights.

The Rise of Transgender Communities

The establishment of transgender groups and support networks marked the beginning of a new era of solidarity and empowerment. We honor transgender pubs, clubs, and safe spaces as places of inclusion and tolerance. These groups have fostered a sense of belonging and resilience in transgender people through hardships and accomplishments.

Transgender Representation in Media and Arts

Transgender portrayal in the media and arts has evolved, challenging preconceptions and encouraging understanding. We investigate the influence of transgender characters in film, television, literature, and art, as well as the works of transgender artists and creatives who have reinvented their identities via their creativity.

The Fight for Transgender Rights and Legal Struggles

We see key judicial decisions that have affected the fight for equality around the world as we dive into transgender rights and legal struggles. The difficulties encountered by transgender people in various countries highlight the necessity of global collaboration and knowledge exchange in building understanding and acceptance.

Understanding Gender Identity and Medical Interventions

The study of gender identity and medical interventions enables us to comprehend the complexities of self-discovery as well as the ethical debates surrounding gender-affirming care. We applaud medical advances that have enabled transgender people to realize their true selves.

Global Perspectives on Transgender Experiences

Our voyage concludes with an examination of global perspectives on transgender lives, with a particular emphasis on cultural attitudes, problems, and achievements in various locations. The transformative power of knowledge sharing and worldwide collaboration emerges as a transforming force in cultivating understanding and progressing transgender equality.

Embracing Diversity, Empowering Change

Our trek through transgender history is a celebration of the tenacity, determination, and development of transgender communities worldwide, in the spirit of embracing difference and empowering change. The instructive and cheery tone represents the hope and optimism that fuels our mission to make the world a more open and compassionate place.

A Call to Transcend Boundaries

As we engage on this transformative path, we are called to cross societal, cultural, and personal barriers. Let us approach this investigation with open hearts and minds, celebrating the uniqueness of each individual as well as the power of collective action in crafting a better, more inclusive tomorrow.

We will celebrate our accomplishments, learn from our mistakes, and remember those who have paved the way for transgender visibility and equality. May this trip through transgender history inspire us to be change agents, equality advocates, and acceptance champions.

Our journey begins now, and with each page flip, we embrace the stories of pioneering individuals, the information imparted by campaigners, and the transformational power of accepting diversity. Join us as we embark on "Transcending Boundaries: A Journey Through Transgender History," a journey that will celebrate resilience, encourage understanding, and empower change for future generations.

Chapter 1: Ancient Notions of Gender

Ancient Notions of Gender: Indigenous Perspectives on Gender Identity

Gender has been a complicated and multidimensional part of identity from the dawn of time. As we go into the annals of history, we discover that ancient tribes all around the world had profound and diverse understandings of gender, often embracing a considerably more inclusive stance than many modern societies do now. In this chapter, we go on a fascinating investigation of ancient concepts of gender, with a particular emphasis on indigenous viewpoints on gender identity.

- **Embracing Gender Diversity:** Indigenous civilizations all around the world have long recognized and celebrated gender variety. Many indigenous communities recognized a spectrum of genders rather than rigid binary categories, recognizing the fluidity and distinctiveness of human identity. Individuals who embodied both male and feminine attributes, for example, were venerated among the Two-Spirit people of several Native American tribes for their unique abilities and views. These people were important members of their societies, typically functioning as healers, spiritual leaders, and wisdom keepers.

- **Gender as Sacred:** Gender was regarded sacred in many traditional belief systems, intricately tied to spirituality and the natural world. It was a heavenly gift given upon individuals by higher forces, not just a social construct. Gender blending was viewed as a manifestation of the interconnection of all living entities and a testament to the universe's balance. Such appreciation for gender variety generated a strong sense of acceptance and respect within these communities, creating a secure space for people to discover and express their true selves.

- **Gender Rituals and Rites of Passage:** Indigenous civilizations frequently performed rituals and rites of passage to mark key life milestones, including those connected to gender identity. These ceremonies are intended to validate and affirm a person's gender expression, providing them with a sense of belonging and purpose in their community. Rites of passage are frequently transformative experiences that guide people on their journey of self-discovery and understanding.

- **Transcending Boundaries:** The concept of "transcending boundaries" is inherent in many indigenous societies' approach to gender. Rather than restricting individuals to predetermined roles based on their biological sex, these communities respected the human capacity to embrace and embody multiple gender identities. This acceptance enabled people to live authentically and find fulfillment outside of traditional conventions.

Reflecting on these old gender conceptions from indigenous viewpoints reveals interesting lessons that resonate with our present knowledge of gender identity. These societies exemplify the transformative potential of accepting, celebrating, and recognizing different gender presentations. Their historical wisdom points us in the direction of navigating the difficulties of gender identification in modern times, establishing an inclusive and compassionate society in which everyone can transcend borders and embrace their true selves.

We will come across more extraordinary examples of endurance, activism, and development as we travel across transgender history. Each chapter will shed more light on the bravery and tenacity of individuals and societies throughout history who have strived to break free from societal restraints and embrace their true selves.

Let us continue our educational and joyful journey through transgender history, appreciating the diversity of human experiences and celebrating the successes of individuals who have paved the way for a more inclusive world. As we progress through the chapters, we will learn about the lives of transgender trailblazers, legal difficulties and victories, medical advances, and global perspectives on transgender experiences. Each chapter is a monument to the indomitable human spirit, a reminder that we are all interconnected and that by crossing barriers, we may construct a brighter and more peaceful future for future generations.

Ancient Notions of Gender: Historical Gender Variance in Cultures Around the World

Gender has been significantly more complicated and diverse throughout human history than our modern understanding generally admits. As we embark on this illuminating trip through transgender history, we shed light on the rich fabric of historical gender variation seen in cultures across the world. Ancient societies honored a kaleidoscope of gender manifestations and identities, rather than rigid binary concepts of gender. In this chapter, we dig into the enthralling stories of historical gender variation, revealing how our forefathers welcomed and cherished the complexities of human identity.

- **Gender Roles and Norms Reimagined:** Contrary to the widely held belief that ancient societies firmly adhered to binary gender standards, several cultures displayed a more fluid and expansive understanding of gender roles. Individuals known as "Hijra" in South Asia and "Two-Spirit" among Native American tribes, for example, existed in many African communities. These people occupied distinct roles in their cultures, frequently combining masculine and feminine traits. They were revered for their unique ideas and played critical roles as healers, spiritual leaders, and cultural information keepers.

- **Gods and Goddesses of Gender Diversity:** Gender diversity was not only acknowledged but also revered in mythology and folklore. Gods and goddesses who rejected standard gender norms abound in ancient pantheons, reflecting the varied character of human identity. From the androgynous deities of ancient Egypt, such as Isis and Osiris, to the gender-fluid characters of Norse mythology, such as Loki, these divine creatures expressed the complexity and fluidity of gender in ways that their respective cultures truly valued.

- **Cultural Perspectives on Gender Diversity:** Gender diversity was embraced as a natural component of human existence across continents, from the Indian subcontinent to Polynesia. The Hijra group of India, which dates back to ancient times, has a distinct social and cultural identity. Polynesian societies acknowledged and embraced the "Fa'afafine" in Samoa and "Mahu" in Hawaii for their distinct gender expressions. Far from being sidelined, these people frequently occupied prominent positions in their societies.

- **Rituals and Celebrations of Gender Variance:** Gender diversity was celebrated rather than stigmatized in many communities. Individuals' gender identities were honored and validated through rituals and ceremonies. For example, in Native American tribes, Two-Spirit people went through elaborate rites of passage to symbolize their distinct roles in the community. These rituals were used to develop a sense of belonging and acceptance as well as to validate gender identity.

We get a profound respect for the complexity of human experience and the boundless possibility of gender expression as we reflect on historical gender variance in civilizations around the world. These historical narratives question present gender norms and remind us that variety has always been a part of the human tapestry.

We will encounter more compelling stories of trailblazers who broke cultural standards, legal challenges and successes, medical developments, and worldwide perspectives on transgender experiences as we continue our trip through transgender history. Each chapter will focus on the tenacity, bravery, and determination of individuals and communities who have led the road to a more inclusive society.

Let us learn from history and enjoy the richness of human diversity. Gender diversity in ancient cultures teaches us that mankind has always been a mosaic of identities, and that by crossing barriers, we may create a society where everyone is valued and accepted for who they are.

Our journey through transgender history is a monument to those who have dared to question conventional standards, as well as a light of hope for a future in which all persons can live authentically and with pride. As we continue this instructive and cheerful journey, may we find inspiration in the stories of the past to construct a brighter, more inclusive future for future generations.

Ancient Notions of Gender: Transgender Figures in Mythology and Folklore

We are transported back to ancient times as we start on an enthralling voyage through transgender history, where the realms of mythology and folklore abound with stories of varied gender identities. Transgender individuals have long graced the chronicles of societies around the world, and they are far from a new concept. Let us begin by going into the enthralling worlds of mythology and folklore, revealing the transcendent stories of transgender people who have broken standard gender boundaries and inspired generations with their stories.

- **The Androgynous Deities of Ancient Egypt:** Egyptian mythology distinguishes out among the ancient pantheons for its depiction of androgynous deities. Osiris, the deity of the afterlife and resurrection, was frequently portrayed as a figure with both male and feminine characteristics. His marriage to the goddess Isis showed the profound union of male and feminine elements, signifying the underlying duality and balance in all things. This divine image of gender diversity served to affirm and legitimate various gender manifestations in Egyptian society.

- **The Shapeshifting Norse God, Loki:** Loki, the mischievous deity in Norse mythology, violated gender boundaries with his shapeshifting skills. Loki, known for his mischievous temperament, could shift forms at will, frequently transforming into different genders. His gender fluidity contradicted the conservative standards of the time, and his stories mirrored Norse culture's acceptance and appreciation of gender diversity.

- **The Transcendent Gender of Ardhanarishvara:** Ardhanarishvara, the Hindu god, depicts the harmonious union of male and female forces. Ardhanarishvara is portrayed as a celestial entity divided in half, with one half representing Lord Shiva and the other half representing his bride, Goddess Parvati. This image not only celebrates the masculine and feminine harmony, but it also embraces the intrinsic flux of gender identity, emphasizing that the divine incorporates all forms of gender.

- **The Amazons: Warriors Beyond Gender Boundaries:** In Greek mythology, the Amazons were a clan of powerful and skillful warrior women who existed outside of traditional gender roles. These powerful women bucked conventional norms by rejecting traditional conceptions of femininity and embracing strength and independence. The stories of the Amazons challenged the concept that war strength and leadership were primarily male attributes, demonstrating the infinite potential of humans regardless of gender.

We are reminded of the ongoing power of narrative to affect views and attitudes about gender as we immerse ourselves in these ageless tales about transgender individuals in mythology and folklore. These historical tales serve as mirrors reflecting the acceptance and appreciation of gender diversity within their different civilizations, rather than simply providing amusement.

Our trip through transgender history demonstrates that transgender identities have always existed, transcending time and culture. These tales and legends show that the human experience has always been as varied as the stars in the sky, and gender identity has always been an important element of that kaleidoscope.

We will discover more amazing stories of trailblazers who pushed society norms, legal challenges and successes, medical developments, and worldwide perspectives on transgender experiences as we continue our investigation. Each story is a testament to the tenacity, bravery, and dedication of individuals and communities that have worked to improve transgender rights and visibility.

Let us honor transgender people in mythology and folklore as icons of bravery, optimism, and perseverance. Their stories transcend the boundaries of time and continue to inspire us now. We can create a more inclusive world where everyone's unique expression is welcomed and appreciated if we recognize and embrace the multiplicity of gender identities.

Our journey through transgender history is a monument to those who have paved the path for progress, as well as a beacon of hope for a future in which all individuals can live authentically and with pride. As we continue on this instructive and uplifting journey, may we find inspiration in old myths and folktales to create a brighter, more inclusive future for future generations.

Ancient Notions of Gender: Gender Diversity in Ancient Societies

We find ourselves transported back to the ancient world, where gender was defined in ways that surpassed the binary concepts prominent in many current civilizations, as we embark on an interesting trip through transgender history. This section delves into the interesting issue of gender variety in ancient societies, looking at how our forefathers accepted and celebrated the complexities of human identity.

- **Beyond Binary: Embracing Gender Spectrums:** Unlike the rigid binary framework that dominates most of contemporary gender thinking, many ancient societies recognized a range of gender identities. From the Hijra community in South Asia to Native American tribes' Two-Spirit people, these societies recognized and valued persons who existed outside of the usual male-female divisions. They celebrated the great diversity of human expression rather than imposing limiting categories.

- **Inclusive Roles and Contributions:** Gender variety was not only recognized, but also integrated into different elements of life in ancient communities. People who represented various gender identities played essential roles in their communities, bringing their distinctive abilities and viewpoints. For example, among Two-Spirit people, their dual nature was generally regarded as a blessing, granting spiritual insight and the capacity to bridge multiple realms within their tribes.

- **Spiritual and Sacred Dimensions:** Gender was interwoven with spirituality and the holy in many ancient cultures. Gender diversity was viewed as a reflection of divine creativity rather than something to be concealed or suppressed. Individuals who had both male and feminine attributes were viewed in some communities as representing the divine duality, reflecting the harmonious balance of conflicting forces in the cosmos.

- **Cultural Celebrations of Gender Diversity:** Ancient communities celebrated gender diversity via festivals and rituals. These celebrations were filled with joy and acceptance, and individuals were recognized for their distinct identities. Such events strengthened the notion that gender variety was a necessary and fundamental element of the human experience.

Reflecting on ancient societies' historical embracing of gender variation reminds us of the richness of human experience and the various possibilities of gender expression. These cultures show that the concept of gender as a fixed and binary construct is a comparatively modern occurrence, and that a more fluid and inclusive understanding of gender existed for much of human history.

Our trip through transgender history illustrates that various gender identities have always existed, transcending time and culture. Gender diversity is an ancient concept that challenges the view that gender is a simple binary, emphasizing that it is a complex and multifaceted component of human identity.

As we continue our exploration, we will encounter more inspiring stories of trailblazers who defied societal norms, legal struggles and triumphs, medical advancements, and global perspectives on transgender experiences. Each chapter illuminates the courage, resilience, and determination of individuals and communities who have contributed to the progress of transgender rights and visibility.

Chapter 2: Transgender Trailblazers in History

<u>Transgender Trailblazers in History: Pioneering Transgender Activists and Advocates</u>

As we travel through transgender history, we meet a plethora of daring and trailblazing individuals who have challenged society standards, opened the way for advancement, and advocated for the rights and visibility of transgender people. This chapter focuses on trailblazing transgender activists and advocates who have worked boldly for equality, understanding, and acceptance.

- **Christine Jorgensen: A Trailblazing Transformation:** Christine Jorgensen, born George William Jorgensen Jr., is regarded as one of the first publicly transgender people to undergo sex reassignment surgery in the United States. She traveled to Denmark in 1952 to undergo the surgery, and upon her return to the United States, she bravely shared her experience with the world. Christine's candor and advocacy helped to demystify transgender experiences and dispel common myths about gender identity.

Aside from her personal effect, Christine Jorgensen was instrumental in establishing medical and legal acceptance for transsexual people. Her transition sparked debate on the medical and psychological elements of gender dysphoria, resulting in more research and knowledge in the field of transgender healthcare. As a result, she became an inspiration to many people who were battling with their gender identity, bringing hope and visibility to a long-marginalized and misunderstood community.

Her boldness and advocacy paved the path for future activists and transgender rights campaigns as well. By bravely revealing her story, Jorgensen attracted attention to the difficulties that transgender people endure, leading to a larger fight for equality and acceptance. Her contribution to transgender history cannot be emphasized, as she contributed to launch a transformation in cultural perceptions toward gender identification and lay the framework for the global growth of transgender rights.

- **Marsha P. Johnson: A Force for Change:** Marsha P. Johnson was a transgender activist and self-identified drag queen who was a significant figure in the LGBTQ+ rights movement. She was a key figure in the 1969 Stonewall Uprising, which represented a watershed moment in the fight for LGBTQ+ rights. Marsha co-founded the activist organization Street Transvestite Action Revolutionaries (STAR), which provide assistance and shelter to homeless transgender and gender nonconforming kids. Her continuous action and advocacy continue to inspire future activists.

Marsha's legacy in transgender history will go on because she was instrumental in bringing to light the challenges that transgender people, particularly transgender persons of color, confront. Her bravery, resilience, and steadfast commitment to justice have inspired generations of activists to fight for equal rights and acceptance of all gender identities. Marsha P. Johnson's legacy lives on as a symbol of courage and a motivating force in the ongoing fight for transgender rights and equality. Her achievements not only benefited the lives of transgender people, but also made an indelible effect on the larger movement for social justice and human rights.

- **Sylvia Rivera: A Champion for the Marginalized:** Sylvia Rivera, a transgender Latina activist, was another pivotal role in the Stonewall Uprising. She co-founded STAR with Marsha P. Johnson to address the needs of homeless transgender and LGBTQ+ youth. Sylvia was a prominent advocate for the community's most marginalized individuals, fighting relentlessly for transgender rights and inclusion within the larger LGBTQ+ movement.

- **Lou Sullivan: Breaking Barriers with Visibility:** Lou Sullivan was a trailblazing transgender homosexual man who was instrumental in campaigning for transgender men's acceptance and inclusion within the LGBTQ+ community. He established the FTM support group to create a safe area for transgender guys to interact, share stories, and offer support to one another. Lou's work helped to raise awareness and understanding of transgender guys and the issues they confront.

FTM International assisted individuals in navigating the difficulties of self-discovery and acceptance. Furthermore, the organization's lobbying work helped to dispel social preconceptions and misconceptions about transgender identities, opening the way for a more informed and compassionate understanding of gender variety. FTM International's legacy is defined by its contributions to defining transgender healthcare, encouraging inclusivity, and empowering numerous transgender men to openly and proudly embrace their true self.

Lou Sullivan was also essential in shifting medical and psychological ideas on transgender healthcare. He was influential in campaigning for more comprehensive care for transgender people, particularly those transitioning. His work aided in the development of a more informed and compassionate approach to transgender healthcare, emphasizing the need of gender identity affirmation.

We are reminded of the significance of visibility and storytelling in effecting social change as we reflect on the lives and achievements of these trailblazing activists and champions. Their willingness to share their stories challenged preconceptions, debunked myths, and humanized the transgender experience.

Our trip through transgender history reveals that these trailblazing advocates aided in the advancement of transgender rights and visibility. They paved the way for future activists and campaigners, sparking a global movement toward greater acceptance and inclusion.

We will discover more amazing examples of individuals who have defied society standards, legal challenges and successes, medical developments, and worldwide perspectives on transgender experiences as we continue our investigation. Each chapter honors persons who have contributed to the growth of transgender rights and social justice through their perseverance, tenacity, and persistence.

Let us continue the work of these trailblazing transgender activists and advocates to create a society where everyone is cherished and appreciated for who they actually are. Their commitment to social change reminds us that one person's advocacy may have a huge impact on the lives of many people.

Our journey through transgender history is a monument to those who have paved the path for progress, as well as a beacon of hope for a future in which all individuals can live authentically and with pride. As we continue this instructive and cheerful journey, may we find inspiration in the fortitude of the past to create a brighter, more inclusive tomorrow for future generations.

Transgender Trailblazers in History: Notable Transgender

<u>Individuals in Pre-modern History</u>

As we embark on this illuminating trip through transgender history, we discover the incredible stories of people who transcended the constraints of their period and embraced their true gender identities. While modern understandings of gender variation have progressed greatly, it is critical to remember that famous transgender individuals have existed since the dawn of humanity. Let us cast a light on some of pre-modern history's trailblazing transgender persons who bravely lived their truth in communities that frequently misunderstood and rejected them.

- **The Warrior Empress, Hatshepsut:** Hatshepsut bucked customary gender stereotypes by coming to the throne as Pharaoh in ancient Egypt. She seized the title of Pharaoh and reigned with wisdom and strength, breaking the gender barrier to become one of Egypt's most successful and important kings. Her reign was highlighted by prosperity and cultural improvements, demonstrating women's authority and capacity in the face of traditional expectations.

- **The Japanese Courtesan, Takatsuru:** Takatsuru, also known as Torii Kiyonobu in feudal Japan, was a well-known kabuki actor and onnagata (a male actor who specialized in feminine roles). Takatsuru's performances as a woman were known for their grace and honesty, winning her audiences' adoration and respect. His artistry and passion questioned gender conventions and highlighted the artistic freedom that allowed people to express their different gender identities on stage.

- **The Transgender Saint, Joan of Arc:** Joan of Arc, a French peasant girl, played a major role in the Hundred Years' War in the 15th century. Joan wore male armor and commanded the French army to multiple triumphs, believing herself to be guided by divine voices. Her bravery and leadership shattered gender stereotypes and demonstrated the indomitable spirit of a young lady eager to define her own destiny.

- **The Renaissance Artist, Caterina de Viviani:** Caterina de Viviani, often known as La Mora, was a talented painter and poet in 16th-century Italy. Caterina was born a man but lived as a woman during the Renaissance period, where she was recognized for her creative abilities. Despite societal constraints that aimed to limit her expression, Caterina's love of art and her female identity enabled her to overcome obstacles and leave her mark on history.

We are reminded that the human experience has always been diverse and multifaceted as we look into the lives of these noteworthy transgender individuals from pre-modern history. Their stories dispel the myth that gender diversity is a recent phenomenon and underline transgender people's long presence throughout history.

Our voyage through transgender history demonstrates that in pre-modern times, these trailblazers bucked cultural standards and paved the way for future generations. Despite enormous hurdles and biases, they displayed endurance, courage, and drive to live genuinely.

Transgender Trailblazers in History: The Hidden Stories of Gender-Nonconforming Figures

As we continue on this enthralling voyage through transgender history, we unearth the hidden stories of gender-nonconforming people whose contributions to society have frequently been eclipsed by the dominant norms of their period. These trailblazers bravely lived above conventional expectations, breaking gender stereotypes and inspiring future generations.

- **The Enigmatic Chevalière d'Éon:** The Chevalière d'Éon, also known as Charles d'Éon de Beaumont, was a 17th-century French diplomat, spy, and swordswoman. Having been designated male at birth, d'Éon spent the majority of her life presenting as a man before recognizing her gender identification. Despite societal constraints, she fought gender norms and embraced her own self throughout her extraordinary life. Her reputation as a skilled diplomat and a courageous individual calls into question gender stereotypes and stresses the complexity of identity.

D'Éon's legacy lives on as a symbol of gender exploration and the fight for gender self-determination, having had a long-lasting impact on the understanding and acceptance of transgender identities throughout history.

- **The Daring Billy Tipton:** Billy Tipton was a jazz musician who rose to prominence in the twentieth century. Tipton was assigned female at birth but lived as a man throughout his adult life. Despite suffering obstacles as a result of his gender identity, Tipton persevered and rose to prominence as a skilled jazz guitarist and conductor. His tale shines light on the struggles and achievements of gender nonconforming people in the entertainment industry, as well as the tenacity required to pursue one's ambitions truthfully.

- **The Fearless Lucy Hicks Anderson:** Lucy Hicks Anderson was a transgender African American woman who lived in the early twentieth century. Lucy, who was assigned male at birth, lived her life as a woman and became a popular socialite and community leader. Despite persecution and prejudice, she bravely embraced her identity, inspiring others to accept and respect her for who she was. Lucy's tale calls into question the assumption that gender expression is constrained by cultural norms, emphasizing the importance of authenticity and self-acceptance.

Even though Lucy Hicks Anderson's life was mostly neglected and erased from historical archives, her legacy has resurrected as the transgender rights movement has gained traction. She is today recognized as a trailblazer in transgender history, a monument to the tenacity and endurance of transgender people who have struggled for recognition, respect, and equality throughout history. Her legacy continues to inspire future generations of transgender activists, encouraging better knowledge and compassion for the transgender community's unique experiences.

- **The Visionary Sir Lady Java:** Sir Lady Java, born William Marchand, was a skilled entertainer and performer in the mid-twentieth century. She refused to disguise her identify and went on to become a significant person in the LGBTQ+ rights movement.

Sir Lady Java opposed discriminatory legislation and advocated for the rights of gender nonconforming people through her activism and performances. Her pioneering initiatives helped to raise awareness and understanding of gender diversity.

We are reminded of the enormous impact that these individuals have had on influencing public attitudes and breaking down gender preconceptions as we reflect on the hidden stories of gender-nonconforming characters. Their experiences demonstrate the bravery and perseverance required to live genuinely in a world that frequently misunderstands and marginalizes individuals who oppose the status quo.

We will discover more amazing stories of trailblazers who have defied society standards, legal challenges and successes, medical developments, and worldwide perspectives on transgender experiences as we continue our investigation. Each chapter honors the perseverance and achievements of those who have influenced the advancement of transgender rights and visibility.

Our journey through transgender history is a monument to those who have paved the path for progress, as well as a beacon of hope for a future in which all individuals can live authentically and with pride. As we continue this instructive and cheerful journey, may we find inspiration in the fortitude of the past to create a brighter, more inclusive tomorrow for future generations.

Transgender Trailblazers in History: Transgender Figures in the Arts and Literature

Transgender people have bravely expressed their identities via many artistic forms throughout history, leaving an indelible influence on culture and society. We honor the trailblazing transgender figures in the arts and literature who have improved the world with their ingenuity and sincerity in this section of the book.

- **The Poetic Vision of Audre Lorde:** Audre Lorde, a notable African American poet, essayist, and activist, left an indelible mark on literature. Lorde, who was open about her lesbian sexuality and her experiences as a Black woman, tackled topics of gender identity in her poetry. Her poems explored the nuances of gender expression and the difficulties that persons who do not comply to cultural standards encounter. Lorde's creative voice was a catalyst for change, inspiring others to embrace their unique identities and speak their truth passionately.

- **The Captivating Novels of Virginia Woolf:** Virginia Woolf, a well-known British author, is remembered for her innovative books that questioned traditional narrative forms and explored themes of identity and gender. Although Woolf's own gender identity is a point of contention among academics, her works frequently address the fluidity of gender roles and the intricacies of human identity. Woolf cleared the ground for talks about gender diversity and gave readers a view into the vast tapestry of human experience through her thought-provoking prose.

- **The Transformative Art of Frida Kahlo:** Frida Kahlo, the renowned Mexican artist, had a significant impact on transgender history, despite not identifying as transgender herself. Her bold and unapologetic approach to gender and identity challenges traditional norms and has resonated deeply with transgender individuals.

Kahlo's art often explored themes of gender fluidity, challenging the binary concepts of femininity and masculinity. She presented herself in a way that defied societal expectations, embracing both feminine and masculine elements in her appearance and self-expression. By doing so, Kahlo paved the way for discussions about gender nonconformity and self-identity.

Her art and life story have served as an inspiration to many transgender artists and people. Kahlo's bravery in expressing her truth, grief, and emotions via her work continues to resonate with underrepresented communities, including transgender people, serving as an inspiring example of self-acceptance and empowerment. Frida Kahlo's art has had a lasting impact on transgender history, challenging stereotypes and developing a more inclusive understanding of gender and identity.

- **The Playwright Pioneering: Terrence McNally:** Terrence McNally, a prolific American playwright, used his works to explore issues of gender identity, sexuality, and the human condition. His play "Some Men" explores the lives of gay men throughout history, addressing the complications of gender presentation and cultural expectations. McNally's plays provided a forum for nuanced and authentic portrayals of LGBTQ+ persons, shattering prejudices and building understanding.

Reflecting on the achievements of transgender figures in the arts and literature, we are reminded of the immense importance of artistic expression in altering attitudes and generating crucial conversations. These trailblazers have utilized their artistic abilities to challenge conventional standards, promote diversity, and campaign for social change.

Our trip through transgender history reveals that the arts and literature have been powerful platforms for transgender people to communicate their tales and experiences with the rest of the world. Their genuineness and ingenuity have enriched society and opened minds and hearts to the beauty of gender diversity.

We will discover more amazing stories of trailblazers who have defied society standards, legal challenges and successes, medical developments, and worldwide perspectives on transgender experiences as we continue our investigation. Each chapter honors the perseverance and achievements of those who have influenced the advancement of transgender rights and visibility.

Let us recognize the transforming potential of transgender artists and writers in the arts and literature. Their work has opened the path for a better appreciation, acceptance, and celebration of gender diversity.

The journey we've taken through transgender history is a monument to those who have paved the path for progress, as well as a beacon of hope for a future in which every person can live authentically and with pride. As we continue this instructive and cheerful journey, may we find inspiration in the artistic representations of the past to create a brighter, more inclusive future for future generations.

Chapter 3: Transgender in the Victorian and Edwardian Era

Transgender in the Victorian and Edwardian Era: The Emergence of Medicalization and Pathologization

As we begin this enlightening tour through transgender history, we will focus on the Victorian and Edwardian eras, which saw tremendous societal upheavals and shifting attitudes toward gender identity. The concept of transgender identity began to emerge during this time period, but it was met with medicalization and pathologization. This chapter explores the complex nature of this historical era, offering insight on the medical opinions and societal attitudes that affected transgender people's lives.

The Victorian and Edwardian eras, which lasted from the late 1800s through the early 1900s, were characterized by social conservatism and rigid gender conventions. The dominant gender views and societal expectations were thoroughly anchored in binary frameworks, leaving little room for nonconforming expressions. As people began to express their gender identities outside of established conventions, medical experts and society as a whole struggled to comprehend and categorize these experiences.

- **Medicalization of Transgender Identity:** Medical and psychiatric practitioners attempted to identify and diagnose individuals who did not fit to standard gender roles during the Victorian and Edwardian eras. In medical literature, terms like "sexual inversion" and "gender dysphoria" began to arise, reflecting the medicalization of transgender identity. These medical viewpoints, however, frequently pathologize gender diversity, depicting it as a mental condition rather than acknowledging it as a valid manifestation of human variation.

- **Early Pioneers in Gender Exploration:** Despite medicalization and pathologization, there were Victorian and Edwardian-era individuals who fearlessly explored and expressed their gender identities. Figures like Michael Dillon, who sought gender-affirming medical therapy in the mid-twentieth century, and Ernest Boulton and Frederick Park, dubbed the "Fanny and Stella" of Victorian England, lived their lives authentically and shamelessly, upsetting traditional standards in the process.

- **Artistic and Literary Reflections:** Gender and identity-related artistic and literary manifestations emerged during the Victorian and Edwardian eras. In their works, writers such as Oscar Wilde and Virginia Woolf gently addressed themes of gender nonconformity and fluidity. These artistic representations were significant reflections of the changing perceptions toward gender throughout this time period.

As we contemplate the medicalization and pathologization of transgender identity during the Victorian and Edwardian eras, we are reminded of the significance of knowing historical context when evaluating the experiences of transgender people. While these beliefs may appear archaic and destructive in today's world, they provide vital insights about the progress achieved in recognizing and affirming gender diversity.

Transgender in the Victorian and Edwardian Era: Unveiling the Lives of Transgender People in 19th-Century Society

The nineteenth century was distinguished by a tight adherence to binary gender standards, with society expectations defining precise roles for men and women. Any divergence from these principles was seen with suspicion and, in many cases, censure. Transgender people found themselves in unknown territory in this atmosphere, battling with their true selves in a world that strove to repress any variation from the norm.

- **Private Journeys of Self-Discovery:** Many transgender people embarked on their journeys of self-discovery in privacy during a time when discussing gender identity was mainly forbidden. Their names and experiences were kept secret from society, with only a few trusted confidantes privy to them. Despite popular belief, these individuals seek to discover and express their genuine selves, finding consolation in embracing their authentic gender identities.

- **Challenges and Triumphs:** The nineteenth century brought enormous obstacles for certain transgender people, as they suffered societal rejection, discrimination, and sometimes legal penalties for their gender expression. Despite these difficulties, there were some victories. Some found supportive networks or were able to navigate gender roles more quietly, allowing them to live more genuinely. Their bravery and drive opened the path for succeeding generations to openly and shamelessly accept their identities.

- **Artistic Expressions of Gender Identity:** Despite cultural limits, some transgender people developed inventive ways to show their gender. They gently addressed topics of gender nonconformity and identity through art, literature, and performance. During a time when open discussions about gender identity were rare, these artistic works provided glimpses into the lives and experiences of transgender people.

When we reminisce on the lives of transgender people in the Victorian and Edwardian eras, we are reminded of their endurance and strength. In a period when gender-nonconforming people were typically suppressed and marginalized, they silently made their own paths, affirming their actual selves in the face of public pressure.

Our stroll through transgender history highlights that transgender people faced both problems and triumphs throughout the nineteenth century. While the dominant beliefs of the time aimed to suppress gender variety, these individuals displayed an extraordinary ability to accept their genuine selves in the face of hardship.

Transgender in the Victorian and Edwardian Era: Early Medical Approaches to Gender Identity

As we continue our fascinating voyage into transgender history, we will look more into the Victorian and Edwardian eras, which were distinguished by conservative cultural norms and rigid gender roles. Within this setting, the advent of early medical treatments to gender identity took center stage, affecting transgender people's understanding and perception at the time. Exploring the medical ideas that emerged in the nineteenth century gives light on the complexity of gender identity medicalization.

Throughout the Victorian and Edwardian eras, there was an increasing interest in analyzing and categorizing human behavior through medical and scientific lenses. Medical practitioners strove to analyze and categorize gender-nonconforming persons' experiences as they questioned societal conventions. As a result, medical ideas and terminologies aiming to explain gender variety emerged.

- **The Concept of "Sexual Inversion":** The concept of "sexual inversion," proposed by sexologist Havelock Ellis, was one of the early medical approaches to gender identification. Ellis felt that certain people experienced a reversal of sexual inclinations, where they were drawn to people of their own biological sex rather than those of the opposite sex. This theory aimed to explain same-sex attraction and included gender nonconforming individuals in its purview, albeit such experiences were pathologized as departures from the norm.

- **The Work of Karl Heinrich Ulrichs:** Karl Heinrich Ulrichs, a German writer and jurist, was an early campaigner for the rights of homosexuals and gender nonconforming people. He coined the term "Urning" to characterize those who had same-sex attraction or had gender-nonconforming behaviour. Ulrichs' study questioned popular belief at the time, claiming that gender variance was a natural and unchangeable component of human experience.

- **The Emergence of "Gender Dysphoria":** The term "gender dysphoria" first appeared in medical literature in the late nineteenth century. This word was coined to express the anguish felt by people whose gender identification did not match their assigned sex at birth. While the notion accepted certain gender-nonconforming people's psychological pain, it still pathologized their experiences as mental diseases.

We appreciate the historical context's intricacies as we reflect on early medical treatments to gender identity in the Victorian and Edwardian eras. These medical ideas arose at a period of conservative beliefs and binary gender understandings, which shaped how gender variety was perceived and classified.

Our tour through transgender history illustrates that the medicalization of gender identity in the nineteenth century was rooted in the prevalent beliefs and societal conventions of the time. While these early tactics may appear antiquated and destructive in retrospect, they provide vital insights into the progress achieved in recognizing and affirming gender diversity.

We are going to uncover more amazing stories of trailblazers who have defied society standards, legal challenges and successes, medical developments, and worldwide perspectives on transgender experiences as we continue our investigation. Each chapter honors the perseverance and achievements of those who have influenced the advancement of transgender rights and visibility.

Transgender in the Victorian and Edwardian Era: Resisting Oppression - Transgender Resilience in the Era of Secrecy

As we resume our enlightening journey through transgender history, we turn our attention to the Victorian and Edwardian eras, a period marked by stringent societal norms and the marginalization of gender variety. Transgender people displayed incredible endurance as they handled the difficulties of their gender identities during this period of concealment and injustice. We should all commemorate the strength and courage of transgender people who stood up to oppression and embraced their authentic selves despite the obstacles they faced.

The Victorian and Edwardian eras were characterized by firmly rooted cultural expectations of binary gender norms, which left limited room for gender nonconforming displays. In such circumstances, transgender people frequently find themselves dealing with their identities in silence and seclusion. Fear of societal rejection, prejudice, and even legal consequences drove many people to hide their true identities from the public.

- **A Hidden Identity:** Transgender people generally led clandestine lives at an era when open discussions about gender identity were uncommon. The seclusion they chose was a sort of self-preservation, acting as a barrier against the dominant attitudes that aimed to suppress gender variation. Their seclusion, however, represented the harsh nature of the society they lived in, which pushed them to hide in the shadows.

- **Quiet Acts of Defiance:** Despite widespread oppression, transgender people engaged in subtle acts of disobedience, finding methods to express their gender identities and connect with others in safe areas. Some people sought consolation and camaraderie in private gatherings, forming support networks that provided understanding and acceptance. These small gestures of rebellion demonstrated their tenacity and bravery in the face of hardship.

- **Surviving and Thriving:** Transgender people developed methods to not only survive but also thrive in the face of societal discrimination. Some were able to navigate gender roles by expressing themselves as genuinely as they could within the confines of the time. Others sought peace and liberation via artistic expression, literature, and performance, gently addressing topics of gender identification.

Transgender history demonstrates that the Victorian and Edwardian eras were a time of both suffering and perseverance for transgender people. Their resolve to embrace their actual selves in the face of adversity demonstrates the enduring power of honesty and self-acceptance.

Chapter 4: The Rise of Transgender Communities

We have arrived at a watershed moment, marked by the creation of transgender communities and support networks. Transgender people discovered strength in unity in the face of adversity and rejection, forming ties that would pave the way for increased visibility, acceptance, and empowerment. In this chapter, we celebrate the rise of transgender communities as well as the tremendous influence of support networks on the trajectory of transgender history.

- **The Stonewall Uprising and Beyond:** The Stonewall Uprising, which occurred in New York City in June 1969, was a watershed point in the history of the LGBTQ+ rights movement, particularly its impact on transgender history. In reaction to a police raid targeting the LGBTQ+ community, the Stonewall Inn, a prominent gay bar in Greenwich Village, became the location of a series of spontaneous protests and rallies.

- The transgender rights movement gained traction in the years following Stonewall. Activists such as Sylvia Rivera continued to push for the rights of transgender and gender nonconforming people, highlighting the intersections of race, gender, and sexuality in their fight for equality.

The significance of the Stonewall Uprising in transgender history cannot be emphasized. It was a watershed moment that galvanized the LGBTQ+ community and rallied transgender people to seek recognition, respect, and equal rights. The fight for transgender rights, visibility, and inclusion owes much to the bravery and resolve of those who resisted at Stonewall and those who followed in their footsteps. The Stonewall Uprising's legacy continues to inspire continuing attempts to establish a more equal and inclusive society for all gender identities.

- **Formation of Advocacy Groups:** Following Stonewall, advocacy groups specializing in transgender rights began to develop. Organizations such as the National Transsexual Counseling Unit (NTCU) and the National Transsexual Action Committee (NTAC) played critical roles in providing transgender individuals with support and resources, advocating for legal and social change, and fostering a sense of belonging within the transgender community.

- **Support Networks and Safe Spaces:** The growth of transgender communities included the establishment of support networks and safe spaces where people may find acceptance and understanding. communal centers, transgender support groups, and social organizations provided important locations for people to share their experiences, battle isolation, and foster a feeling of communal pride.

- **The Impact of Media and Literature:** The emergence of transgender communities was also aided by media coverage and literature. Leslie Feinberg's "Stone Butch Blues" and Leslie Feinberg and Kate Bornstein's "Trans Liberation: Beyond Pink or Blue" presented transgender stories to a wider audience, building a sense of solidarity and understanding. Documentaries and films portraying transgender people aided in raising awareness and understanding.

The establishment of these communities represented a watershed moment in transgender history, propelling the movement forward with renewed vigor and tenacity. These networks' connections and sense of belonging have provided a lifeline to countless transgender people, encouraging them to live authentically and confront societal boundaries.

Each chapter honors the perseverance and achievements of those who have influenced the advancement of transgender rights and visibility. Their united strength, activism, and devotion to one another serve as motivation to continue developing a world in which all individuals can live with respect and inclusion.

As we continue this instructive and optimistic journey, may we find inspiration in the unity and resilience of the past to build a brighter, more inclusive future for future generations.

The Rise of Transgender Communities: Transgender Bars, Clubs, and Safe Spaces

In the face of societal hurdles and discrimination, these venues played a transforming role in developing supporting networks and celebrating the diversity of gender identity.

- **Transgender Bars as Sanctuaries:** Transgender bars arose as havens of acceptance and fellowship for people seeking sanctuary from a world that frequently misunderstood and marginalized them. These locations gave clients a sense of safety and belonging, allowing them to express themselves without fear of judgment or prejudice. Transgender bars became valued havens, providing reprieve from the difficulties of navigating a culture still coping with gender variety.

- **Clubs as Centers of Celebration:** Transgender nightclubs and nightlife establishments became places of celebration and affirmation. Individuals could relish in their identities in these bright venues, surrounded by a community that understood and supported them. The exuberance of the dance floor, as well as the sense of brotherhood established in these venues, created an environment of joy and pride, which helped to counteract the weight of societal prejudice.

- **Support and Community Building:** Transgender pubs, clubs, and safe spaces were essential for community growth. They provided venues for support groups, social gatherings, and educational programs, allowing people to share their experiences and knowledge. As transgender people banded together to confront discriminatory legislation and pursue equality, these venues became incubators for activism, advocacy, and mutual empowerment.

- **Creating Visibility and Challenging Stereotypes:** Transgender pubs and clubs also played an important part in increasing transgender visibility. These venues fought damaging assumptions and misinformation about gender identity by existing openly and proudly. They demonstrated the multiplicity of experiences among the transgender community, dispelling myths and building understanding.

You are reminded of the power of community in breaking down barriers and encouraging social change as you research the relevance of transgender pubs, clubs, and safe spaces. These locations acted as beacons of hope, encouraging transgender people to embrace their identities and find strength in community.

The Rise of Transgender Communities: Challenges and Triumphs in Building Transgender Communities

As individuals created relationships and developed a feeling of belonging in the face of adversity, the growth of these communities was distinguished by both obstacles and achievements. Everyone should celebrate transgender people's persistence and tenacity in creating communities that have molded transgender history.

- **Navigating Prejudice and Discrimination:** Building transgender communities has been a difficult task, since transgender people have experienced prejudice and discrimination from society at large. The widespread stigma associated with gender variation has frequently resulted in rejection, violence, and exclusion. Despite these obstacles, transgender people persevered, realizing the need of finding like-minded companions and providing safe settings for them to thrive.

- **Overcoming Isolation:** Many transgender people have felt isolated and lonely, particularly in societies that lack knowledge and acceptance of gender variety. Creating communities was a lifeline for those striving to break free from the bonds of solitude. They found refuge in shared experiences and established ties that fostered personal growth and empowerment by joining together.

- **Creating Safe Spaces:** One of the victories in the development of transgender communities has been the creation of safe spaces where people may be themselves without fear of condemnation or injury. Transgender support groups, community centers, and internet forums have provided venues for mutual support, affirmation, and activism. These places have become safe havens for transgender people to celebrate their identities freely and truthfully.

- **Collective Empowerment:** Transgender communities have served as catalysts for collective empowerment, allowing people to band together and lobby for their rights. Transgender communities have used activism and advocacy to protest discriminatory policies, seek legal protections, and demand social acknowledgment. The power of togetherness has moved the movement ahead, resulting in positive change for transgender people all around the world.

The experience of constructing these communities illustrates the power that comes from finding one's voice and standing together as a unified force. Transgender people have demonstrated that, when united, they can transcend borders and overcome difficulties, from the early days of secret and quiet to the birth of vibrant communities. Their communities serve as beacons of hope and empowerment, fostering a society in which gender diversity is celebrated and appreciated.

The Rise of Transgender Communities: Trans Activism in the Mid-20th Century

In the mid-twentieth century, we have arrived at a watershed moment, marked by the establishment of transgender communities and the birth of transformative trans activism. Transgender people banded together to demand recognition, equality, and rights in the face of adversity, discrimination, and societal ignorance. Discover the impact of trans activism on the trajectory of transgender history.

- **Visibility and the Fight for Recognition:** Trans activism in the mid-twentieth century was marked by a concerted effort to raise attention and demand acknowledgment. Activists tried to combat the erasure and obscurity of transgender experiences, claiming the right to be seen, heard, and valued. They began to build areas where transgender voices could not be silenced through protests, campaigning, and community organizing.

- **The Compton's Cafeteria Riot:** The Compton's Cafeteria Riot occurred in San Francisco in 1966, three years before the historic Stonewall Uprising. Transgender and queer people, who are frequently ostracized and harassed by police, revolted against injustice, resulting in several nights of protests. The uprising was a forerunner of transgender resistance to injustice and police abuse.

- **Activism for Legal Protections:** Transgender activists realized the critical need for legislative safeguards in the mid-twentieth century. They battled for cross-dressing to be decriminalized and for the opportunity to receive identification documents that appropriately matched their gender identity. They established the framework for future legal achievements in transgender rights through their campaigning.

- **Healthcare Advocacy and Access:** Transgender activists also fought extensively to increase access to healthcare. They battled against discriminatory policies that denied transgender people basic medical care, and they worked to de-pathologize gender variance in medical discourse.

We are constantly reminded of the bravery and tenacity of people who defied conventional standards and paved the road for development. Their activity illustrates the strength of collective action as well as the tenacity of individuals who refused to be silenced. This era's advocacy laid the groundwork for the revolutionary advances in transgender rights and visibility that are still taking place today. Each chapter honors the perseverance and achievements of those who have influenced the advancement of transgender rights and visibility. Their legacy is a tribute to transgender people's tenacity and resilience in their pursuit of equality and acknowledgment.

Chapter 5: Transgender Rights and Legal Struggles

Transgender Rights and Legal Struggles: Landmark Legal Cases for Transgender Rights

There are numerous crucial moments in the film that go into the legal battles and landmark decisions that have established transgender rights. Following prejudice and structural hurdles, transgender people and activists have gone to the courts to demand equality, acknowledgment, and legal protection. We commemorate the victories of these important judicial decisions in this chapter, which have improved transgender rights and opened opportunities to greater inclusivity.

- **The Case of Michael Dillon (1949):** The Case of Michael Dillon, which occurred in 1949, was a watershed point in transgender history. Michael Dillon, a British physician, requested gender confirmation surgery in order to live freely as a male. Dillon undertook a series of procedures to transition with the assistance of Sir Harold Gillies, a pioneering plastic surgeon.

His story drew attention to transgender issues and generated debates regarding gender identity and medical therapies for transgender people. Despite the cultural stigma and inadequate medical understanding at the time, Michael Dillon's fearlessness in openly pursuing his genuine self-broke conventional norms and preconceptions.

Michael Dillon's case had a huge impact on medical viewpoints on transgender healthcare. His experiences, as well as Sir Harold Gillies' surgeries, aided in the increasing understanding of gender dysphoria and the medical treatments available to assist transgender people.

Furthermore, Michael Dillon's story acted as an inspiration for many transgender people who were grappling with their identities. His journey of self-discovery and acceptance gave hope and visibility to a long-marginalized and misunderstood community.

- Michael Dillon's quest for authenticity, as well as the medical procedures he experienced, paved the door for increased acceptance and understanding of transgender identities. His influence on transgender history is indisputable, as he helped to pioneer a shift in society attitudes toward gender identity and contributed to the ongoing fight for transgender rights and acceptance.

- **Reed v. Reed (1971):** Reed v. Reed, while not strictly a transgender rights case, was a seminal Supreme Court decision that established the essential premise of "strict scrutiny" for gender-based classifications. This idea was later important in promoting transgender rights by requiring a compelling state interest in gender-based discrimination.

- **M.T. v. J.T. (1999):** After her divorce, a transgender woman named M.T. sought joint custody and visiting rights for her children in this pioneering lawsuit. The court's decision acknowledged her as a parent, establishing a significant precedent for transgender parental rights.

- **Renaissance Holdings v. DHS (2004):** In this landmark decision, the United States District Court found that a transgender woman's transition-related healthcare must be funded by Medicaid since refusing such coverage violated the Equal Protection Clause.

- **Obergefell v. Hodges (2015):** While most remembered for establishing national marriage equality, the momentous Supreme Court decision in Obergefell v. Hodges also lay the groundwork for transgender rights recognition. The judgement underscored the significance of equal legal protection and dignity for all people, regardless of sexual orientation or gender identity.

- **G.G. v. Gloucester County School Board (2017):** Gavin Grimm, a transgender high school student, sued his school board for the right to use the restroom that corresponded to his gender identity. Even though the case was later remanded to lower courts, it spurred global debates over transgender rights and restroom access.

- **Bostock v. Clayton County (2020):** The decision in the Bostock v. Clayton County case by the United States Supreme Court in June 2020 had a profound impact on transgender history. The case addressed the problem of sex discrimination in the workplace and its ramifications for LGBTQ+ employees, particularly transgender people.

The Supreme Court ruled in a landmark decision that Title VII of the Civil Rights Act of 1964 protects LGBTQ+ employees from discrimination based on sexual orientation and gender identity. This ruling was a significant step forward in recognizing the rights of transgender people in the workplace.

The court's ruling in Bostock v. Clayton County not only created critical legal safeguards for transgender employees, but it also delivered a powerful message recognizing the dignity and equality of all LGBTQ+ people. The verdict aided in the elimination of discriminatory practices and promoted a more inclusive and accepting work environment for transgender people throughout the United States. It is a big step forward in the ongoing fight for transgender rights, and it has established a precedent for future court battles over LGBTQ+ equality and acceptance.

Each case is a historical turning point in the ongoing fight for transgender equality and legal recognition. Advocates and individuals have fought relentlessly to remove discriminatory barriers and obtain safeguards for the transgender community as a result of these historic cases. More inspiring stories of trailblazers who have pushed society norms, legal difficulties and victories, medical advances, and worldwide perspectives on transgender experiences will be shared. These cases provide hope and inspiration for a future in which transgender people can live truthfully and with dignity, free of discrimination and prejudice.

Transgender Rights and Legal Struggles: The Fight for Recognition and Protection

We are currently at an important stage in the fight for transgender rights and legal recognition. In the face of societal hurdles and discrimination, transgender people and activists have bravely gone to court to demand equality, dignity, and legal protection.

- **The Power of Visibility:** The power of visibility has spurred the campaign for transgender rights. As transgender people came forward to share their tales and experiences, assumptions and misconceptions were demolished. The growing visibility of transgender life in the media, arts, and public settings has been critical in fostering empathy and understanding.

- **Challenging Discrimination:** Transgender people and campaigners have been at the forefront of the fight against discriminatory laws and practices. They have battled for anti-discrimination safeguards in areas like as employment, housing, healthcare, and education through major legal battles and grassroots lobbying. Their initiatives have helped to secure stronger legal protections for transgender people.

- **The Evolution of Legal Precedents:** Legal precedents have changed throughout time to recognize transsexual rights. As evidenced by major instances such as Bostock v. Clayton County, courts have acknowledged that discrimination based on gender identity is a type of sex discrimination. These legal triumphs have established critical precedents that protect transgender people from discrimination.

- **Parental Rights and Recognition:** Another critical battleground has been the fight for transgender parental rights. Legal triumphs in instances such as M.T. v. J.T. have established transgender parents' right to be acknowledged and respected in custody and visitation disputes, reinforcing their position as loving and caring parents.

- **Transgender Rights in Healthcare:** Advocates have made great progress in ensuring transgender people's healthcare rights. Cases such as Renaissance Holdings v. DHS have highlighted the need of providing comprehensive and gender-affirming healthcare, as well as lowering obstacles to essential medical care.

- **Transgender Rights in Education:** The fight for transgender rights in education has focused on topics such as toilet access and anti-discrimination legislation in schools. The case of G.G. v. Gloucester County School Board shows transgender kids' courage and commitment in pushing for their rights.

The recent success demonstrates the transformative potential of collective action and the belief in a more inclusive future. Transgender persons have challenged discriminatory policies and gained legal safeguards that have improved the lives of countless others via court triumphs, advocacy, and community support.

We will discover more amazing stories of trailblazers who have defied society standards, legal challenges and successes, medical developments, and worldwide perspectives on transgender experiences as we continue our investigation. The triumphs are proof of the steadfast belief in a world where transgender people are recognized, protected, and appreciated for who they are.

Transgender Rights and Legal Struggles: Challenges to Health Care and Employment Equality

Transgender people and advocates have worked relentlessly to remove discriminatory barriers and secure their rights in the search of recognition and protection. Let us explore through the significant legal battles that have defined transgender rights in health care and employment, while also celebrating the unwavering spirit of resilience and hope.

- **The Fight for Health Care Equality:** Transgender people have always faced substantial barriers to equitable health care. Many insurance companies have previously denied coverage for transgender-related care, creating significant barriers to gender-affirming medical treatments and procedures. However, significant advances in health care equity for transgender people have been made as a result of major court cases and lobbying campaigns.

- **The Affordable Care Act (ACA) and Transgender Protections:** The ACA, which was passed into law in 2010, contains important safeguards for transgender people. The Act made it illegal for insurance companies to reject coverage or charge higher premiums based on gender identification. These safeguards were a huge step forward in ensuring transgender people have equitable access to health care.

- **The Struggle for Employment Equality:** Employment discrimination has caused significant obstacles for the transgender community. Prejudice, intolerance, and a lack of understanding have resulted in the denial of job chances, unjust workplace treatment, and even termination based on gender identification. Advocates and activists have championed employment equality through legal action and public awareness initiatives.

- **Bostock v. Clayton County and Employment Protections:** The United States Supreme Court declared in Bostock v. Clayton County, in a landmark decision, that discrimination based on sexual orientation and gender identity is forbidden under Title VII of the

Civil Rights Act. This historic judgment extended federal employment protections to transgender people, establishing an important barrier against discrimination.

- **Creating Safe and Inclusive Workplaces:** Aside from legal successes, several firms have taken proactive initiatives to make transgender employees' workplaces safe and inclusive. Companies have policies and training programs in place to encourage diversity, equity, and inclusion. These efforts have resulted in a beneficial shift in workplace culture, resulting in increased acceptance and understanding.

- **Addressing Health Disparities:** Transgender people have also experienced inequities in mental health treatment and medical services. Many people have been discouraged from obtaining medical care due to stigma and discrimination, resulting in health disparities within the community. Advocates have sought to increase awareness of these difficulties and increase access to transgender-affirming mental health care.

The advancements in these areas highlight the transformative potential of legal action and collective determination. These legislative triumphs, together with ongoing initiatives, have paved the way for a future in which transgender people can live truthfully and without fear of prejudice. These accomplishments demonstrate the transformative power of collective action and the persistent hope for a more inclusive and equitable future.

Transgender Rights and Legal Struggles: Intersectionality and the Fight for Equality

Gender identification is merely one aspect of the fight for equality; it also overlaps with racial, economic, and disability issues. Transgender people from all walks of life have encountered unique challenges, and their perseverance in the face of discrimination and prejudice has been inspiring.

- **Transgender Rights and Racial Equity:** As racial discrimination combines with gender identity prejudice; transgender people of color frequently confront increased challenges. Advocates for transgender rights have always emphasized the need of racial equity and justice. Recognizing and responding to the distinct experiences of transgender people of color has been critical in building a more inclusive movement.

- **The Impact of Economic Barriers:** Economic inequalities have also had a substantial impact on transgender experiences. Transgender people with lower means have been disproportionately disadvantaged by workplace discrimination, limited access to education, and healthcare hurdles. Legal battles have been waged to rectify economic imbalances and achieve economic justice for all.

- **Legal Challenges for Transgender Refugees and Immigrants:** Transgender refugees and immigrants have encountered a series of legal obstacles that are specific to them. Many people have sought asylum to avoid persecution because of their gender identity or nationality. Advocates have worked hard to ensure that transgender refugees and immigrants are treated fairly and have access to legal safeguards.

- **The Disability Intersection:** Individuals with disabilities may face hurdles to getting gender-affirming healthcare and accommodations, therefore their rights intersect with transgender rights. Advocates have stressed the significance of legislative safeguards recognizing and addressing the intersections of disability and gender identity.

- **Transgender Advocacy in the Criminal Justice System:** Transgender persons, especially transgender people of color, have been subjected to disproportionate levels of violence and mistreatment in the criminal justice system. Advocates have worked for systemic improvements to guarantee that transgender people are treated fairly and have their rights protected in the criminal justice system.

- **Creating Inclusive Spaces:** Intersectional advocacy has also focused on building welcoming environments and resources for transgender people. Community centers, support organizations, and healthcare providers have attempted to serve transgender people's different needs, considering the intersectional problems they may experience.

Recognizing and responding to the unique realities of transgender people from various origins has been critical in furthering the rights of everyone. The interdependence of these concerns has been highlighted through intersectionality, resulting in a more comprehensive and inclusive approach to lobbying. In order to continue this instructive and uplifting journey, we must find inspiration in the resilience of the past to create a brighter, more inclusive tomorrow for future generations.

Chapter 6: Exploring Gender Identity and Medical Interventions

Exploring Gender Identity and Medical Interventions: Understanding Gender Dysphoria and Medical Diagnosis

Exploration of gender identity and medical interventions is an important element of understanding about transgender and gender identity history. The experience of gender dysphoria has been a transformational component of many transgender people's lives. Understanding the complexity of gender identity and the medical procedures involved is critical for developing empathy and informed conversations.

- **Gender Identity and Authenticity:** Gender identity is fundamental to a person's sense of self. Gender dysphoria is commonly experienced by transgender people when their gender identification does not match the sex given to them at birth. Accepting one's true gender identity is a transformative path of self-discovery and self-acceptance.

- **Understanding Gender Dysphoria:** Gender dysphoria is the anguish felt by people whose gender identity differs from their assigned sex at birth. This misery can take many forms, including emotional and psychological discomfort. Understanding and recognizing gender dysphoria is essential in giving support and compassionate care to transgender people.

- **The Importance of Medical Diagnosis:** Gender dysphoria medical diagnosis is an important stage in the process of gender-affirming care. It assists healthcare practitioners and individuals in navigating the complications of transitioning and obtaining necessary medical interventions. A diagnosis can also help with insurance coverage and legal acknowledgment of gender identification.

- **Informed Consent Model:** Many healthcare professionals have embraced an informed consent paradigm that emphasizes the significance of patient autonomy and agency in making gender-affirming medical decisions. Individuals are the authorities on their own gender identity and requirements; therefore this paradigm eliminates unneeded gatekeeping barriers.

- **Medical Interventions for Gender-Affirming Care:** Gender-affirming medical procedures have the potential to significantly reduce gender dysphoria and improve the well-being of transgender people. Hormone therapy, gender-affirming procedures, and other medical therapies tailored to an individual's specific needs are examples of these interventions.

- **Mental Health and Support:** Mental health support is essential in the care of transgender people. Mental health experts play an important role in giving emotional support, affirmation, and assistance with transitioning and gender identity discovery.

Understanding gender dysphoria and how it is diagnosed medically allows us to approach the subject with empathy, respect, and care. Transgender people have increased access to gender-affirming care and assistance as society becomes more educated and accepting. The road of self-discovery and gender affirmation demonstrates the power of accepting one's true identity.

Exploring Gender Identity and Medical Interventions: Historical Perspectives on Hormone Therapy and Surgeries

Transgender people's lives have been changed by a significant advancement in medical care, particularly in the fields of hormone therapy and surgery. Understanding the historical perspectives on these treatments is critical to appreciating the progress made and the transformative influence on the lives of transgender people.

- **Historical Context of Gender-Affirming Care:** Transgender people have long sought ways to reconcile their physical bodies with their gender identification. While medical therapies have been around for centuries, the acceptance and availability of gender-affirming care has developed throughout time.

- **Early Medical Interventions:** According to historical sources, several ancient cultures, such as the Indian Hijra society and different indigenous societies, recognized the existence of people with distinct gender identities. While not comparable to modern hormone therapy and surgery, these communities embraced distinct gender roles and expressions.

- **The Emergence of Hormone Therapy:** The twentieth century saw considerable advances in hormone therapy for transgender people. The first documented hormone treatments began in the 1930s, largely employing estrogen for feminizing effects. These early advances paved the way for more extensive hormone regimens.

- **Harry Benjamin and the Standards of Care:** Dr. Harry Benjamin, an endocrinologist, was instrumental in lobbying for transgender medical care. He established the Standards of Care, which offered a foundation for gender-affirming care by establishing rules for hormone therapy and operations.

- **Surgical Interventions:** Surgical procedures have been a game changer in gender-affirming care. Some transgender people sought procedures in the mid-twentieth century, but they faced major obstacles due to social stigma and medical gatekeeping.

- **The Stonewall Uprising and Activism:** The Stonewall Uprising, a watershed moment in LGBTQ+ history, spurred a wave of action and advocacy for transgender rights in 1969. During this time, the visibility and demand for medical care expanded, pushing more medical practitioners to specialize in gender-affirming procedures.

- **Advancements in Surgical Techniques:** As medical knowledge grew, so did surgical approaches for gender-affirming procedures. Technique and technology advancements have resulted in more effective and safer surgeries for transgender people.

- **Inclusion and Accessibility:** There has been a drive in recent decades for greater inclusion and accessibility of gender-affirming care. Advocates have pushed to de-stigmatize these medical interventions and make them available to everyone who require them.

- **The Power of Personal Stories:** Personal tales of transgender people seeking gender-affirming care have played an important role in raising awareness and promoting understanding throughout history. In society, the sharing of experiences has promoted empathy and compassion.

Their road to honesty and acceptance has had a revolutionary impact on transgender history. Medical advances and increasing campaigning have contributed to a more accepting and friendly environment for transgender people. The advancement of medical therapies demonstrates the power of acceptance and the desire of authenticity.

Exploring Gender Identity and Medical Interventions: Ethical Debates and Medical Advances in Gender-Affirming Care

Gender-affirming care's evolution has not been without ethical disputes and hurdles. Medical advances and increased understanding, on the other hand, have prepared the path for revolutionary change in delivering compassionate and competent treatment for transgender people. We arrive at ethical considerations and medical discoveries in gender-affirming care, honoring the transgender community's perseverance in seeking true expression.

- **Ethical Considerations in Gender-Affirming Care:** The pursuit of gender-affirming care has created significant ethical concerns, including as informed consent, age-appropriate interventions for children, and assuring patient-centered and empowering care.

The implementation of an informed consent paradigm has been a huge step forward in gender-affirming care. This paradigm values patient autonomy by allowing individuals to make educated decisions about their medical care without the need for unnecessary gatekeeping.

- **Age-Appropriate Interventions for Minors:** Transgender minors' medical treatment has been the topic of ethical discussion. While some support puberty blockers and hormone therapy for minors, others are concerned about long-term repercussions. Medical standards emphasize the significance of customized care that considers the minor's physical and mental well-being.

- **Mental Health Support:** In gender-affirming care, the ethical consideration of mental health assistance is paramount. It is critical to provide individuals with access to mental health experts who are informed with gender identity difficulties in order to promote favorable outcomes.

  Some ethical discussions revolve around the possibility of regret in gender-affirming care. According to studies, many transgender people who receive medical treatment report better well-being and happiness with their gender identity.

- **The Role of Medical Professionals:** The role of medical practitioners in providing gender-affirming care is also the subject of ethical discussion. Many people believe that in order to deliver the most complete and compassionate care, healthcare personnel should be trained in transgender health.

- **Promoting Inclusivity:** Ethical concerns have also prompted a movement for more diversity in gender-affirming care. Recognizing and addressing the distinct needs of transgender people from various backgrounds is critical to fostering equitable treatment.

- **Medical Advances in Gender-Affirming Care:** Medical science has made major advances in gender-affirming care, making therapies for transgender people safer and more effective.

- **Hormone Therapy Advancements:** Hormone therapy has experienced significant advances in dosing regimens, administration systems, and formulations, providing individuals with more personalized options to meet their specific needs.

Gender-affirming surgery techniques have grown to become more complex and precise. Technological advancements and medical expertise have improved surgical results and shortened recuperation times.

- **Inclusive Research:** Ethical reasons have also driven more inclusive transgender health research. Medical studies are now attempting to incorporate varied demographics in order to better understand the unique experiences of transgender people.

The advancement of gender-affirming care ethics has produced a more inclusive and supportive atmosphere for persons seeking authenticity and acceptance. The continual dedication to medical progress and inclusivity highlights the transforming power of recognizing and affirming one's gender identity. The path to authenticity and acceptance demonstrates the power of compassion and progress in creating a more inclusive world.

Exploring Gender Identity and Medical Interventions: The Impact of Medical Interventions on Transgender Lives

Medical procedures have had a dramatic effect on transgender people's lives, allowing them to embrace their true selves and live satisfying lives.

- **Gender-Affirming Hormone Therapy:** Hormone therapy has long been a cornerstone of gender-affirming care for transgender people. Transmasculine men may experience physical changes like as voice deepening, body hair growth, and muscular development as a result of testosterone medication. Estrogen therapy can cause breast development, changes in body fat distribution, and skin softening in transfeminine people. These physical changes can help an individual's physique align with their gender identification, leading to enhanced confidence and well-being.

- **Surgical Interventions for Gender Affirmation:** Transgender people have experienced life-changing alterations as a result of gender-affirming surgeries. Chest masculinization, vaginoplasty, phalloplasty, and facial feminization surgery have helped people feel more at ease with their gender identity. These surgical treatments have improved not only physical health, but also mental health and overall well-being.

Medical interventions have a positive impact on the lives of transgender people that extends beyond physical changes. Many people find hormone therapy and procedures to be incredibly affirming, alleviating gender dysphoria and improving mental health. Accepting one's real gender identity can boost one's self-esteem, reduce anxiety, and provide an overall sense of empowerment.

- **Enhanced Quality of Life:** Medical interventions have enhanced transgender people's quality of life. Gender-affirming treatment enables people to actively participate in career, school, and social activities by reducing gender dysphoria and developing self-acceptance, resulting in a more fulfilling life.
  Medical procedures provide far-reaching benefits that go beyond the individual. Transgender people are becoming more visible and socially accepted as more people adopt gender-affirming care. Because of this growing acceptance, there is more transgender advocacy and understanding in society.

- **Empowerment and Advocacy:** Many transgender people have become champions for transgender rights as a result of the empowerment that comes with gender-affirming care. Their stories of resilience and transformation have inspired others and aided in the advancement of social change.
  Supportive healthcare environments increase the effectiveness of medical interventions. Transgender people feel more safe and comfortable obtaining care when healthcare providers are informed, empathetic, and affirming.

- **Recognizing Individual Journeys:** It is critical to note that the influence of medical interventions differs depending on the individual. Some transgender people may opt not to have medical procedures, which is a fair and respectable choice.

Their paths to honesty and self-acceptance attest to the transformational potential of medical interventions. Transgender people's lives are enriched as gender-affirming care becomes more accessible, and society benefits from greater variety and understanding. Gender-affirming care's transforming effect demonstrates the limitless possibilities of embracing one's actual identity.

Chapter 7: Transgender Representation in Media and Arts

Transgender Representation in Media and Arts: Transgender Characters in Film and Television

Transgender characters in film and television have developed over time, reflecting shifting social attitudes while also giving a platform for increased exposure and understanding. In this chapter, we recognize the transforming significance of transgender representation on transgender life and social perspectives.

- **Early Portrayals and Challenges:** Transgender characters were frequently portrayed in the early years of film and television through negative preconceptions and sensationalized depictions. These erroneous and insulting portrayals reinforced damaging narratives about transgender people, promoting social stereotypes.

- **The Rise of Authentic Storytelling:** In recent decades, there has been a clear shift toward more honest narrative, giving voice to transgender experiences and persons. Filmmakers and television producers have increasingly sought collaboration with transgender authors, performers, and activists to ensure accurate and respectful portrayals.

The introduction of groundbreaking transgender characters onscreen has had a revolutionary effect. Characters like Angel Evangelista in "Pose" and Nomi Marks in "Sense8" have captured audiences' hearts while showing the diverse lives of transgender persons.

- **Transgender Actors in Leading Roles:** The emergence of transgender performers in key roles has marked a tremendous advancement in authentic depiction. Laverne Cox and MJ Rodriguez, for example, have torn down barriers and displayed the skill and nuance of transgender performers.

- **Challenging Stereotypes:** In their search of accurate portrayal, filmmakers and television producers have challenged assumptions and clichés associated with transgender characters. Transgender people's representation has become more sophisticated, stressing their strength, tenacity, and humanity.
Empathy and understanding can be elicited through transgender depiction. Audiences get the ability to connect with transgender characters, gaining a better understanding of the challenges and accomplishments individuals face.

- **Award Recognition and Accolades:** Transgender representation in the media and arts has been recognized with honors and accolades. The recognition of transgender actors and creators attests to the importance of their work.

- **Expanding Diversity:** As transgender representation develops, so does acknowledgement of the transgender community's variety. Transgender characters from varied origins and experiences are featured in stories to help create a more inclusive narrative.

- **Transgender Storytellers behind the Camera:** Transgender persons have made significant gains behind the camera, in addition to greater onscreen representation. Transgender filmmakers, authors, and producers are helping to make transgender experiences more authentic and diverse by sharing their unique perspectives.

Positive transgender characters in film and television have had a social impact, both in terms of cultural growth and challenging societal preconceptions of transgender individuals.

We are captivated by the power of narrative in building empathy and understanding as we reflect on the progression of transgender representation in media and arts. Transgender characters' rising prominence has transformed the narrative surrounding transgender lives, paving the door for a more inclusive and tolerant society. Transgender portrayal continues to expand as society becomes more aware and accepting, creating opportunities for greater authenticity and variety onscreen. Storytelling's power has opened hearts and minds, transcending barriers and promoting a more inclusive and compassionate world.

Transgender Representation in Media and Arts: Transgender Artists and Creatives Redefining Identity

Transgender representation in artistic fields has shattered prejudices and opened up new opportunities for self-expression and understanding. Take in transgender artists' contributions to altering the gender identity narrative.

- **The Power of Artistic Expression:** Art has long been acknowledged as a potent tool for self-expression and social change. Transgender artists have used their artistic ability to challenge social norms and share their personal experiences, fostering empathy and connection.

  Transgender artists have been at the forefront of transforming people's perceptions of themselves. Their work usually reflects the subtleties of gender identification, prompting viewers to ponder on the fluidity and complexities of human lives.

- **Transgender Voices in Literature:** Transgender authors have made great contributions to literature, with dramatic novels delving into the complexities of gender identification, self-discovery, and societal acceptance.

- **Music as a Source of Empowerment:** Transgender musicians have found empowerment through their talent, utilizing music to express their feelings, hopes, and struggles. Their melodies strike a chord with listeners, delivering a sense of consolation and connection.

- **Transgender Artists in Performance Arts:** Transgender actors, dancers, and performers have captivated audiences in the realm of performance arts, demonstrating the power of authentic representation on stage and film.

  Transgender filmmakers and directors have helped to break down barriers and increase transgender visibility onscreen. Their works break traditional storytelling standards by offering new perspectives and stories.

- **Transgender Creatives in Fashion:** Transgender designers and models have emerged in the fashion business, challenging traditional beauty standards and celebrating individuality.

- **Advocacy Through Creativity:** Transgender artists frequently use their platform to advocate for transgender visibility and rights. Their work takes on the role of activism, advocating for a more open and welcoming society.

- **Creating Safe Spaces for Expression:** Transgender artists and creatives have played an important part in providing safe spaces for other transgender people to explore their own creativity and openly express their identities.

- **Collaboration and Solidarity:** Transgender artists frequently cooperate with one another, fostering a sense of togetherness among the community. Their combined efforts boost their advocacy and increase the impact of their work.

They have contributed to a more inclusive and compassionate world via their art and campaigning. Their work has influenced not only the creative professions, but also societal transformation. The power of creativity has no bounds, and transgender artists are continuing to pave the way for better understanding and celebration of varied identities.

Transgender Representation in Media and Arts: The Role of Media in Shaping Transgender Perceptions

Transgender representation in media and the arts has had a significant impact on society attitudes and understanding. The media has played an important part in breaking down barriers and promoting greater acceptance of transgender identities.

- **Early Stereotypes and Misrepresentations:** Transgender people were frequently portrayed in the early years of media through negative preconceptions and misrepresentations. These portrayals contributed to the marginalization of transgender populations by perpetuating misconceptions and stigma.

- **Challenging Misconceptions:** There has been a progressive shift in media depiction in recent decades, with a rising realization of the need to combat prejudices and promote realistic portrayals of transgender people.

- **Humanizing Transgender Characters:** The humanization of transgender characters in film, television, and literature has aided in the development of empathy and understanding. Authentic portrayals allow audiences to connect on a deeper way with transgender realities.

- **Inclusion and Visibility:** Transgender characters' increased acceptance and visibility in media has contributed to a more diverse and representative landscape. Transgender people now have more opportunity to see themselves positively portrayed on film.

- **Transgender Storytellers Behind the Camera:** Transgender authors, directors, and producers in the media have contributed an authentic perspective that has enriched storytelling. Transgender artists add richness and dimension to stories, resulting in more authentic renderings.

- **Documentaries and Non-Fiction Narratives:** Documentaries and nonfiction tales have been significant in shining light on transgender experiences. These stories have the potential to educate, challenge prejudices, and foster understanding.

- **Positive Role Models:** Positive transgender role models in the media have been crucial in pushing people to embrace their true identities. These characters serve as sources of inspiration and empowerment.

- **Addressing Intersectionality:** The media's involvement in addressing intersectionality has been critical in showcasing the multiple experiences of transgender people from various backgrounds, cultures, and identities.

- **The Impact of Transgender Advocacy:** Transgender activists and organizations' advocacy efforts have altered media coverage, resulting in more realistic and empathetic portrayals.

- **Media as a Catalyst for Change:** The ability of media to alter cultural attitudes and encourage societal change is what gives it transformative power. Positive representations can help to fight biases and build a more inclusive society.

The media's influence goes far beyond entertainment; it changes public perceptions and promotes empathy and inclusivity. Positive depictions are becoming more visible, demonstrating the resiliency and activism of transgender populations. Let us recognize the instructive and positive tone that celebrates the progress made in cultivating empathy and understanding as we appreciate the role of media in molding transgender perspectives. The strength of media resides in its ability to cross borders and unify disparate populations through common narratives.

Transgender Representation in Media and Arts: Transgender Stories in Contemporary Literature

Transgender literature has evolved as an important forum for self-expression, understanding, and advocacy. The influence of literature has begun to cross boundaries, strengthening transgender voices.

- **Diverse Narratives:** The complexity of transgender experiences has been embraced in contemporary literature, providing a forum for a diverse spectrum of narratives. These works offer a rich tapestry of transgender life, ranging from coming-of-age stories to stories of resilience and strength.

- **Authentic Voices:** Transgender authors have shaped contemporary literature by infusing their works with honesty and personal knowledge. Their stories elicit empathy and connection from readers.

- **Visibility and Empowerment:** Transgender persons as protagonists in contemporary literature have enabled people to see themselves in stories of success and hardship.

- **Exploring Gender Identity:** Many contemporary literatures explore the difficulties of gender identity, asking readers to consider the challenges of self-discovery and the flexibility of gender presentation.

- **Family and Relationships:** Transgender experiences in literature frequently address topics such as family acceptance, romantic relationships, and friendships, highlighting the significance of supporting and inclusive surroundings.

- **Challenging Stereotypes:** Literature has been a significant weapon in combating damaging stereotypes and misconceptions about transgender people. These works remove bias and encourage understanding through diverse and nuanced portrayals.

- **Youth Literature:** Contemporary youth fiction has been essential in giving young readers with realistic and strong transgender characters, establishing a sense of belonging and affirmation.

- **Intersectionality and Representation:** Transgender stories in modern literature frequently explore intersectionality, recognizing the varying realities of transgender people from various ethnic, cultural, and socioeconomic origins.

- **Transgender Memoirs:** Memoirs written by transgender people have had a profound impact, revealing firsthand experiences of personal hardships, successes, and journeys toward self-acceptance.

- **The Role of Imagination:** Fictional works give a safe environment for creative expression and representation by exploring imagined worlds that transcend the limitations of reality.

These works are beacons of hope, leading readers to a greater knowledge and compassion. The growing prominence of transgender stories in literature demonstrates transgender authors' tenacity and perseverance.

We will come across more amazing stories of pioneers who have defied society standards, legal challenges and successes, medical developments, and worldwide perspectives on transgender experiences as we continue our exploration. We get insight into the complex tapestry of transgender lives through literature, so building a more inclusive and welcoming world.

Chapter 8: Global Perspectives on Transgender Experiences

<u>Global Perspectives on Transgender Experiences: Transgender Rights and Activism Worldwide</u>

Transgender people in various parts of the world have faced unique obstacles and achievements, defining the global growth of transgender rights.

- **Diverse Cultural Perspectives:** Because of differences in cultural attitudes and beliefs, global perceptions on transgender experiences vary substantially. Transgender people have been regarded as spiritual leaders in some civilizations, while they have endured persecution and violence in others.

- **Legal Recognition of Gender Identity:** Transgender rights campaigners have made tremendous progress in campaigning for legal gender identity recognition. Many countries have established legislation that allows transgender people to change their gender marker on official documents, thereby verifying their social identity.

- **Challenges to Legal Recognition:** Despite advances, there are still obstacles in countries where legal acknowledgment of gender identity is limited or non-existent. Transgender activists are still fighting for the right to be legally recognized for their gender identification.

- **Healthcare and Medical Access:** Access to transgender-affirming healthcare remains a global concern. Transgender activists' campaign for better healthcare services, particularly gender-affirming treatments and operations.

- **Violence and Discrimination:** In many parts of the world, transgender people continue to experience violence and discrimination. Transgender rights activists devote their lives to combating discrimination and promoting acceptance.

- **Transgender Rights in Education:** Education is crucial in fostering understanding and empathy. Transgender rights advocates push for inclusive education that takes transgender students' needs into account.

- **Transgender Activism in Non-LGBTQ+ Friendly Regions:** Transgender activists confront considerable hurdles and risks in areas with restricted LGBTQ+ rights. Their bravery and determination in advocating for change is inspirational.

- **International Collaboration:** Transgender rights activists from around the world collaborate to share their experiences, ideas, and resources. International alliances have been critical in promoting transgender rights on a worldwide basis.

- **Online Activism:** The growth of the internet and social media has created a forum for transgender activists to reach a larger audience, rally support, and raise awareness about transgender issues worldwide.

- **Visibility and Representation:** The increased visibility of transgender people and their stories has helped to challenge prejudices and promote understanding.

As we reflect on global perspectives on transgender experiences, we are struck by the tenacious spirit of transgender activists who work tirelessly to create a more open and inclusive world. The success gained in various locations demonstrates the power of lobbying and collaborative effort. Their advocacy crosses boundaries, promoting a more welcoming and caring environment for all.

Global Perspectives on Transgender Experiences: Cultural Attitudes and Acceptance of Gender Diversity

Cultural conventions and beliefs have affected how transgender people are regarded and treated throughout different locations. Investigate the rich tapestry of cultural attitudes toward gender diversity, as well as continuous initiatives to create greater acceptance.

- **Cultural Variations in Gender Norms:** Gender standards are seen differently in different cultures around the world. Some societies tightly enforce binary gender roles, whereas others have long accepted non-binary and gender-fluid identities.

- **Historical Perspectives on Gender Diversity:** Many societies throughout history have recognized and celebrated gender difference. Individuals that did not match typical gender ideals, such as Two-Spirit people in Indigenous cultures, were frequently given positions in ancient society.

- **Transgender Spiritual Leaders:** Transgender spiritual leaders have played important roles in many civilizations throughout history, where their distinct sense of gender and spirituality has been valued and honored. Two-Spirit individuals have been recognized as sacred and respected figures in various Native American tribes, embodying both male and feminine attributes, making them potent conduits between the physical and spiritual realms. The Two-Spirit tradition includes a wide range of functions, such as healers, shamans, and ceremonial leaders. These people are thought to have particular skills and insights because they can embody both male and feminine energies, bridging the gap between the earthly and spiritual realms.

Another example is in South Asia, where hijras have long been recognized as spiritual leaders in certain groups. Hijras are people who do not comply to established gender conventions and are commonly referred to as the "third gender." Hijras are thought to have supernatural powers in some Hindu and Muslim cultures and are asked to conduct blessings during significant life events such as childbirth and weddings. They are also important in certain religious festivals and rituals. Their spiritual presence is said to bring good fortune and prosperity, making them popular figures for spiritual counseling and blessings.

- **Religious and Spiritual Influences:** Religious and spiritual beliefs have a large influence on cultural views about gender diversity. Some religions accept and affirm transgender identities, but others may impose limits or prejudices.

- **Challenges and Progress:** Transgender people may confront acceptance and understanding issues in regions with well ingrained cultural beliefs toward gender. However, there are instances of growth and shifting viewpoints.

- **Family and Community Support:** The experiences of transgender people can be greatly influenced by family and community support. Families in certain cultures are deeply supportive, offering love and acceptance, yet in others, there may be opposition and conflict.

- **Transgender Rights and Legal Recognition:** Cultural attitudes toward gender variety frequently impact the recognition of transgender rights and legal safeguards. Legal recognition may correlate with societal acceptability in progressive nations, but it may be a source of dispute in others.

- **Influence of Globalization:** Globalization has enhanced cultural interchange and awareness of gender diversity around the world. Because of this connection, there have been both problems and opportunities for increased understanding.

- **Education and Awareness:** Education and awareness campaigns are critical in overcoming cultural biases and increasing acceptance of gender diversity.

- **Promoting Intersectionality:** Understanding the interconnectedness of cultural views and gender diversity is critical for creating inclusive workplaces for all people.

The different ways mankind perceives and navigates identity are reflected in each culture's notion of gender. The progress made toward broader acceptance demonstrates the power of education and open debate. Acceptance of gender diversity crosses barriers, creating a more inclusive and compassionate environment for all people.

Global Perspectives on Transgender Experiences: Transgender Movements and Challenges in Different Regions

Let us debate global perspectives on transgender experiences, with a particular emphasis on transgender movements and issues in various locations. The struggle for transgender rights and visibility has been a strong force in determining the global progress of transgender communities.

- **Transgender Activism in North America:** Transgender activism in North America has played a vital role in bringing about significant social and legal reforms for the transgender community. Activists have actively pushed for transgender rights recognition, lobbying for inclusive policies and regulations that defend the dignity and equality of transgender people.

The campaign for legal recognition and protection from discrimination is one significant example of transgender activism's impact. Transgender activists have led initiatives to include gender identity and expression in anti-discrimination legislation at both the state and federal levels. Activists have succeeded in winning legal protections for transgender persons in a variety of areas, including employment, housing, education, and public facilities, through grassroots organization, lobbying initiatives, and public awareness campaigns.

Transgender activists have also played an important role in raising awareness and understanding of transgender issues in North America. Activists have used media campaigns, educational projects, and public speaking engagements to dispel prejudices, combat misconceptions, and encourage empathy and acceptance for transgender people. Their initiatives have increased social awareness of transgender experiences, resulting in better understanding and support for transgender rights and inclusion.

Transgender activism in North America remains a driving force in the continuous fight for equality and social justice, promoting beneficial reforms that benefit not only the transgender community but society as a whole.

- **Transgender Challenges in South America:** Transgender issues in South America show the terrible reality that transgender people confront in the region. Discrimination, violence, and limited access to key services are all frequent issues that have a substantial influence on transgender people's well-being and rights.

Transgender people endure high levels of violence and hate crimes in several South American countries, which are generally motivated by prejudice and ignorance. Transgender people are prone to abuse and marginalization due to a lack of legal protections and understanding of their rights. Furthermore, the societal stigma associated with transgender identities might result in limited educational and employment possibilities, increasing their socioeconomic challenges.

Access to healthcare is another major issue for transgender people in South America. Many people experience barriers to receiving gender-affirming medical procedures, such as hormone therapy and gender confirmation surgery. Transgender populations confront additional challenges due to a lack of qualified healthcare providers and discriminatory practices within the healthcare system.

Despite these difficulties, there are encouraging examples of strong and resilient transgender communities working for change. Transgender activists and groups are working relentlessly across South America to increase awareness about transgender problems, campaign for legal protections, and improve access to healthcare. Organizations such as ANTRA in Brazil and Trans Siempre

Amigas in Colombia, for example, are dedicated to assisting transgender people, offering services, and advocating for their rights and well-being.

The bravery and tenacity of these South American transgender communities and activists serve as a strong reminder of the ongoing fight for equality and human rights. Their initiatives are paving the way for a more welcoming and inclusive society in which transgender people can live freely and without fear of violence or discrimination.

- **Transgender Rights in Europe:** Transgender rights in Europe vary by country, reflecting differing cultural perspectives. Some countries have made tremendous progress in legal recognition, while others continue to confront discrimination and healthcare issues.

- **Challenges in Asia:** In Asia, transgender populations experience varied degrees of acceptance and problems. There are major legal and cultural impediments in some regions, whereas progressive initiatives for transgender rights exist in others.

India is a real-life example of the difficulties that transgender people experience in Asia. Transgender individuals in India have historically endured substantial discrimination and social isolation, notwithstanding recent legal advances. In India, the transgender population has frequently been neglected and subjected to violence and abuse. However, in 2014, the Indian Supreme Court issued a groundbreaking judgement that acknowledged transgender people as a "third gender," allowing them legal status and certain privileges. This decision was a major step in recognizing transgender people's rights in the country, however more work remains to be done to address the broader issues they confront in terms of social acceptance, healthcare, and employment.

- **Transgender Activism in Africa:** Transgender rights activists in Africa are pushing for legislative protections, healthcare access, and recognition. Cultural views and inadequate resources continue to pose challenges.

South Africa is a real-life example of transgender advocacy in Africa. South Africa was the first country in the world to constitutionally safeguard the rights of transgender people in 2003. The Alteration of Sex Description and Sex Status Act, passed by the South African parliament, allows persons to change their gender identity on official papers without undergoing gender confirmation surgery. This innovative legislation was a watershed moment for transgender rights in Africa, laying the groundwork for other countries in the region to follow.

- **Oceania's Transgender Perspectives:** Oceania's transgender experiences vary, with some countries acknowledging and encouraging gender variety, while others face discrimination and insufficient resources.

- **Transgender Rights in the Middle East:** Transgender people confront distinct problems in the Middle East because to cultural conventions and religious beliefs. Despite these difficulties, there are courageous campaigners striving for change.

Iran is an actual example of a transgender rights movement in the Middle East. While Iran's overall LGBTQ+ rights situation remains complicated, the government has established several progressive policies in comparison to other countries in the area. The Iranian government permitted gender confirmation surgery for transgender people in 1987, making it one of the few Middle Eastern countries to do so. They have also permitted people who have had such procedures to change their legal gender on official documents.

- **Collective Global Movements:** Transgender activists from all across the world have joined forces to fight for equal rights and visibility.

The International Transgender Day of Visibility (TDOV) is a real-life example of a global collective movement for transgender rights. TDOV, observed annually on March 31st, strives to promote awareness of the accomplishments and challenges experienced by transgender people, as well as to recognize their contributions to society. On this day, activists and organizations from around the world get together to host events, share stories, and push for transgender visibility and acceptance.

- **Challenges in Healthcare Access:** Access to gender-affirming healthcare remains an issue in many parts of the world, with transgender activists advocating for better medical services and treatments.

- **Addressing Stigma and Discrimination:** Transgender activists throughout the world fight to combat stigma and discrimination while also promoting understanding and acceptance.

Their fortitude in the face of adversity fosters positive change and progress. Progress in some sectors demonstrates the strength of activism and advocacy. Transgender movements' combined strength transcends boundaries, producing a more inclusive and caring world for all persons.

Global Perspectives on Transgender Experiences: Sharing Knowledge - Global Collaboration for Transgender Equality

In today's increasingly interconnected globe, activists, advocates, and communities are banding together to promote awareness, acceptance, and equal rights for transgender people.

- **Knowledge Exchange and Awareness:** The exchange of knowledge, experiences, and best practices in promoting transgender equality is made possible through global collaboration. Activists and groups provide useful information in order to raise awareness and educate communities.

- **International Conferences and Forums:** International transgender conferences and forums allow activists to convene, debate obstacles, and devise solutions. These events build a sense of community and a sense of purpose.

- **Global Advocacy Initiatives:** Collaborative advocacy efforts bring diverse voices together to lobby for legislative reforms, legal recognition, and better healthcare for transgender people.

- **Collective Research Efforts:** Researchers from many regions work together to undertake studies that provide a more comprehensive understanding of transgender lives and issues. This study serves as a foundation for lobbying efforts and policy recommendations.

- **Support for Transgender Activists:** Global partnership provides activists with emotional and financial support in areas where advocating is particularly difficult. Their drive and impact are strengthened by their unity.

- **Transnational NGO Partnerships:** Transnational collaborations between non-governmental organizations (NGOs) allow for the pooling of resources and expertise to address issues that cross national boundaries.

- **Social Media and Digital Activism:** Online platforms help activists communicate globally and expand the reach of transgender equality movements.

- **Translating and Disseminating Resources:** To enable accessibility for diverse populations, activists translate and share educational resources in multiple languages.

- **Addressing Global Health Disparities:** Collaborative initiatives are focusing on tackling health inequities experienced by transgender people around the world, such as HIV/AIDS and mental health difficulties.

- **Educational Exchanges:** Transgender activists and educators collaborate in educational exchanges that encourage cultural understanding and gender diversity.

The global solidarity of activists gives optimism for a more egalitarian and inclusive future. The progress made demonstrates the tenacity and passion of those who collaborate for positive change.

We will encounter more inspiring examples of leaders who have defied society standards, legal difficulties and victories, medical developments, portrayals in media and arts, cultural attitudes toward gender diversity, and regional problems and successes as we continue our investigation. Each chapter honors the perseverance and achievements of those who have influenced the advancement of transgender rights and visibility. We work together to break down barriers and create a society where everyone may live authentically and with dignity.

CONCLUSION

As we come to the end of our illuminating trip through transgender history, we are overwhelmed with awe and inspiration. Each chapter has revealed a tapestry of perseverance, tenacity, and development, ranging from ancient gender concepts to modern transgender activism. We have recognized the contributions of trailblazers who bucked conventional standards, broke down legal barriers, accepted their true identities, and paved the road for greater exposure and acceptance.

Our trip began with an investigation of ancient gender concepts, which offered light on the historical acceptance of gender variation in diverse societies. We learned that gender nonconformity has been woven into the fabric of human history since time immemorial, from revered Two-Spirit folks in Indigenous cultures to the acceptance of transgender figures in mythology and folklore. These stories remind us that recognizing and accepting multiple gender identities is a timeless celebration of human uniqueness.

We witnessed the difficulties and successes of transgender trailblazers who boldly advocated for their rights and visibility as we progressed through history. Their stories have motivated us to break free from the chains of secrecy and stand proud in our truth from the Victorian and Edwardian eras through the mid-twentieth century. We celebrated the birth of transgender groups, their safe spaces, and the difficulties they encountered in creating inclusive surroundings.

We watched major cases that have affected the fight for equality around the world during our examination of transgender rights and legal struggles. The bravery of activists in various places, as well as their coordinated efforts to advocate for change, have taught us the value of collective action. We've seen how cultural attitudes regarding gender diversity influence transgender experiences, but we've also seen how worldwide collaboration and knowledge sharing can build understanding and acceptance.

We rejoiced in the power of storytelling to challenge preconceptions and foster empathy during our trip through transgender representation in media and arts. Transgender characters in film, television, literature, and art have helped to mainstream transgender experiences, producing a more inclusive narrative.

We then descended into the perplexing world of gender identity and medical procedures, gaining an appreciation of the obstacles and achievements of self-discovery and honesty. Medical ethics arguments have inspired us to address the problem with empathy and understanding.

Throughout our investigation, we have seen the transforming potential of education, awareness, and social media in creating understanding and togetherness. Global collaboration has been critical in advancing transgender rights, sharing expertise, and assisting activists in areas where LGBTQ+ rights are limited.

We are reminded of the resiliency of the human spirit and the power of human connection as we reflect on this informative and uplifting journey. We've learnt that the fight for transgender equality isn't limited by geographical or cultural boundaries, but rather is a universal quest for acceptance, respect, and equal rights.

While we celebrate our accomplishments, we recognize that problems remain. Transgender people continue to experience prejudice, violence, and limited access to healthcare and legal recognition in several parts of the world. The road to full equality is not without challenges, but activists' steadfast dedication and the power of global collaboration give us hope for a better future.

Our journey through transgender history demonstrates the value of storytelling and education in creating empathy, breaking down prejudices, and increasing understanding. As we go forward, we must continue to share these experiences, celebrate diversity, and empower change.

As we near the end of this transforming journey, we are filled with optimism and determination. We carry the experiences of the trailblazers, the information imparted by campaigners, and the tenacity of transgender communities around the world with us. Our dedication to building understanding and promoting equality is unwavering.

Let us move forward with compassionate hearts, open minds, and a communal spirit that transcends boundaries. We can work together to build a society where all people, regardless of gender identity, are free from prejudice, embraced by love, and empowered to shine brightly.

May this trip through transgender history inspire us to be change agents, equality advocates, and acceptance champions. Let us chart a course for a more inclusive and compassionate world, where every individual's individuality is acknowledged, and every heart is touched by the transformational power of accepting variety.

As we say goodbye to this informative and uplifting inquiry, may we carry the torch of progress, illuminating the route to a brighter, more inclusive destiny for future generations. We empower change by breaking down barriers.